21st Century Skills **INNOVATION** *Library*

Airplanes

by Nancy Robinson Masters

INNOVATION IN TRANSPORTATION

Published in the United States of America by Cherry Lake Publishing
Ann Arbor, Michigan
www.cherrylakepublishing.com

Content Adviser: Amy C. Newman, Director, Forney Museum of Transportation

Design: The Design Lab

Photo Credits: Cover and page 3, ©egd, used under license from Shutterstock, Inc.; page 4, ©Jemini Joseph, used under license from Shutterstock, Inc.; page 7, ©Vintage Images/Alamy; page 8, ©Sherri R. Camp, used under license from Shutterstock, Inc.; page 11, ©Mary Evans Picture Library/Alamy; page 13, ©iofoto, used under license from Shutterstock, Inc.; page 14, ©Herbert Kratky, used under license from Shutterstock, Inc.; page 16, ©Elena Elisseeva, used under license from Shutterstock, Inc.; page 17, ©Stephen VanHorn, used under license from Shutterstock, Inc.; page 19, ©Gregory Bajor/Alamy; page 21, ©Stephen Strathdee, used under license from Shutterstock, Inc.; page 23, ©History Archive/Alamy; page 24, ©AP Photo; page 26, ©David Gowans/Alamy; page 28, ©Pictorial Press Ltd/Alamy; page 29, ©The Print Collector/Alamy

Library of Congress Cataloging-in-Publication Data
Masters, Nancy Robinson.
Airplanes / by Nancy Robinson Masters.
    p. cm.–(Innovation in transportation)
Includes index.
ISBN-13: 978-1-60279-235-7
ISBN-10: 1-60279-235-6
1. Airplanes–History–Juvenile literature. I. Title. II. Series.
TL547.M352 2009
629.133'34–dc22   2008014582

Cherry Lake Publishing would like to acknowledge the work of
The Partnership for 21st Century Skills.
Please visit www.21stcenturyskills.org for more information.

CONTENTS

INNOVATION IN TRANSPORTATION

CHAPTER ONE

History in Flight

A white-crowned sparrow prepares to fly from a branch. For thousands of years, humans wondered how birds flew.

Whoosh! Wilbur Wright saw a sparrow fly past the window of his bicycle shop one afternoon in 1896.

"What if humans could fly like the birds?" he wondered.

Ancient writings and drawings show that people were asking this question thousands of years before Wright. In the past, most people rarely traveled more than a few miles from where they were born. Walking or riding an animal was the only means they had for travel on land.

Mountains, oceans, and deserts got in the way. Yet these obstacles did not stop tiny sparrows from going where they wanted to go.

People began to explore new ideas. Unfortunately, the very first innovators of flight did not succeed. Their experiments did not produce the results they had hoped for. But they did not stop thinking about ways they could try to fly.

Innovators in China learned how to capture hot air rising from fires in paper bags. They sent the hot air-filled bags over their enemies to frighten them during battles. Scientists in Europe and South America began conducting experiments using hot air to create lift. Lift is a force of energy that pushes something up. Some scientists made claims that they had flown huge sailing ships powered by hot air through the skies.

It wasn't until 1783 that the Montgolfier brothers in France built a hot air balloon that carried two men in a

Learning & Innovation Skills

 An innovator is a person who thinks of a new idea or invention, or discovers a new way to do something. What that person creates is called an innovation. Which of the following do you think are important skills for innovators?

Reading
Studying
Observing
Thinking
Experimenting
Listening
Questioning

If you said all of these skills are important, you are right! Which of these skills do you use the most? Do you have any other skills that will help you be an innovator?

basket beneath the balloon. There was still a big problem. The men floating in the basket did not have a way to control the direction the balloon carried them. The balloon needed something to steer it. That wouldn't be invented for many years.

About 100 years later, airships were carrying passengers. An airship was a balloon with a gondola—or seating cabin—hanging beneath. Ferdinand von Zeppelin of Germany began building huge cigar-shaped airships called dirigibles. His dirigible balloon fabric was wrapped around a stiff, metal frame. These airships were filled with gases such as **hydrogen**, which were lighter than air. These gases helped the airships float. Some people saw these mighty airships as the last flying innovations men would ever build. They were wrong!

In the late 1800s, another German innovator named Otto Lilienthal had a new idea. Lilienthal came up with his idea after reading about a man named Sir George Cayley of England. Sir George performed many experiments with kites. Using Sir George's research, Lilienthal built a glider with fixed wings that did not flap up and down. He made more than 2,000 flights in his willow wood glider covered with wax and cloth. He kept records of each flight.

Which brings us to 1896 and the sparrow flying by Wilbur Wright's window. "What if someone built

a glider with fixed wings that could be controlled by
the person flying it?" he wondered. "What if the glider
also had an engine to give it power?" Suddenly, Wilbur
stopped working. He knew the answer to these questions!

He would build a machine that would make it
possible for a human to fly like a bird!

Special supports were needed to hold the metal
frames of huge dirigibles. These frames were
sometimes called skeletons.

CHAPTER TWO

To the Skies and Beyond

An airplane can drop thousands of gallons of water, mud, or environmentally safe chemicals on wildfires.

What do we need airplanes for? Originally, people were fascinated with the idea of traveling through the air. People wanted to be able to cross the oceans and mountains faster. Today, airplanes **transport** millions of passengers from city to city, state to state, and country to country each year. Airplanes also are used in almost every country to fight fires and to protect crops from diseases and insects. Airplanes carry food and medicine to areas where there are no roads, stores, or hospitals. Veterinarians use airplanes to reach injured animals in need of treatment. Airplanes are even used to search for hurricanes and spray chemicals into clouds to produce rain.

No one thought of these uses when Wilbur and Orville Wright built the first powered, controllable flying machine. They flew their *Wright Flyer* for the first time on December 17, 1903. The Wright brothers thought people would see the importance of their invention. Their idea was for airplanes to be used for peaceful purposes, such as carrying mail and moving people more quickly from place to place. But because the military wanted planes, the Wright brothers also produced "flyers" for the army. They continued to experiment with ways to improve their machine. They focused on building better engines, simpler controls, and adding wheels.

Other innovators in Europe also were building flying machines. Many of them were trying to improve the Wright brothers' design. Louis Bleriot built a flying machine that he hoped would help him travel over water. In 1909, Bleriot flew his machine across the **English Channel**. Immediately, he received more than 100 orders for his "aeroplanes." His flight from France to England changed the way people thought about air travel. They began to see flight as a new way to travel. It started the

Learning & Innovation Skills

Can two people invent the same thing without each other knowing it? Yes! Innovators Frank Whittle of England and Hans von Ohain of Germany each invented a jet engine. Neither of them knew the other had the same idea for an airplane engine that did not need a propeller.

The patent for Whittle's jet engine was issued in 1930. Ohain's jet engine was the first to actually be used on an airplane, in 1939. Even though they did not know each other, the two men had the same idea. However, each arranged the parts of their engines in a different way. Innovators may have the same idea for an invention but use different methods to make their invention work.

What would you do if you had an idea for an invention and learned someone else had the same idea?

race between countries to develop new and better airplane technology.

World War I (1914–1918) showed that airplanes could be used for military combat. For the next 20 years, there were many innovations in designs, shapes, sizes, materials, and engines. During this time, two of the most important innovations in airplane technology occurred: building airplanes with one wing (monoplane) instead of two (biplane), and using metal instead of fabric to cover the framework. Charles Lindbergh used these two innovations to build the *Spirit of St. Louis* airplane. He became the first person to fly an airplane nonstop from New York to Paris in 1927.

Men were not the only ones with new airplane ideas. Sisters Katherine and Marjorie Stinson used innovative ways to teach flying in the United States. They

Metal and fabric were both used to cover the frame of the *Spirit of St. Louis*.

performed in air shows to demonstrate their skills. Katherine amazed audiences by tying fireworks to the wings of her airplane and landing in the dark. Marjorie became known as the "flying schoolmarm." When she was just 19, Marjorie was asked to teach pilots from Canada new ways to fly airplanes in combat. She trained them to make quick dives and climbing turns to avoid becoming the target of enemy planes. She had discovered how to do these dives and turns while flying in air circuses with her sister.

Marie Marvingt of France was the third woman in the world to receive an airplane pilot's license. She flew bomber planes for the French army during World War I. Marvingt thought that airplanes should be used to transport people who needed emergency medical care. Much of her life was devoted to developing air ambulance services around the world.

Hundreds of airplane improvements were made in England, France, Germany, Japan, and the United States during World War II (1939–1945). The most important was the development of the jet engine. The jet engine made it possible for airplanes to fly higher, faster, and farther carrying heavier loads and using less fuel.

More innovations in airplane technology are expected in the 21st century to meet **global** needs. One new airplane is the Boeing 787 Dreamliner. It is being built with hundreds of thousands of parts. These parts are being made in more than 20 different countries. This means people of different **cultures** are working together to produce an airplane that will be flown all over the world. Now that's innovation!

CHAPTER THREE

Outside the Cockpit

The airplane is a terrific example of how one new idea leads to another. With the development of bigger, better, and faster airplanes came innovations in other areas as well.

The first airports were open fields. There were no runways. Airplanes needed smoother surfaces for taking off and landing. In 1901, a British businessman named E. Purnell Hooley discovered how to mix

Paved runways allow smoother take-offs and landings.

gravel and tar to make a product called Tarmac for paving roads. Tarmac later became the first material to pave airport runways. Today, any large paved area at an airport is known as the tarmac.

During the early days of flying, pilots had a tough time flying at night. Pilots got lost when they couldn't see the ground. Paul Henderson, who worked for the U.S. Post Office Department (now known as the U.S. Postal

Pilots use runway lights as guides as they approach for landing.

Service), invented a system of electric lights to help guide airmail pilots flying at night. The lights were set on top of towers built every 10 miles (16 kilometers) across the United States. Airports where the mail planes landed soon were using this idea to show pilots exactly where to land. Airports began using electric lights to outline the runways at night. The airport at Cleveland, Ohio, became one of the first to have paved and lighted runways.

For many years, waiting in airports for flights was a boring experience. Airport builders wanted to make traveling by air more popular and enjoyable. So they built airport **terminal** buildings that featured restaurants, bookstores, and shops. Today, some terminals include shopping centers, movie theaters, skating rinks, swimming pools, and hotels. Internet service is also available in airports, so travelers can communicate globally while waiting for their flights.

As the airports became larger, they needed ways to get people quickly from one location to another. Shuttle buses, automated trains, and moving sidewalks inside terminals are innovations used by millions of passengers each day in airports around the world. All of these inventions help to make airplanes and air travel more convenient.

International airports offer services to travelers from many different countries. Providing language translators, banks for exchanging money, and religious services are just some of the ways international airports meet the needs of people from many cultures.

Some items that were developed for airplanes have found their way into our daily lives. For example, fabrics that don't burn easily were created to make airplanes safer. Manufacturers now use these same fabrics to make safer covers for mattresses, couches, and chairs in our homes.

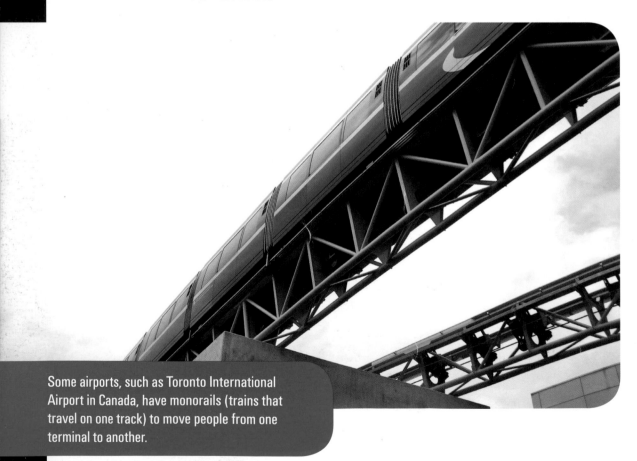

Some airports, such as Toronto International Airport in Canada, have monorails (trains that travel on one track) to move people from one terminal to another.

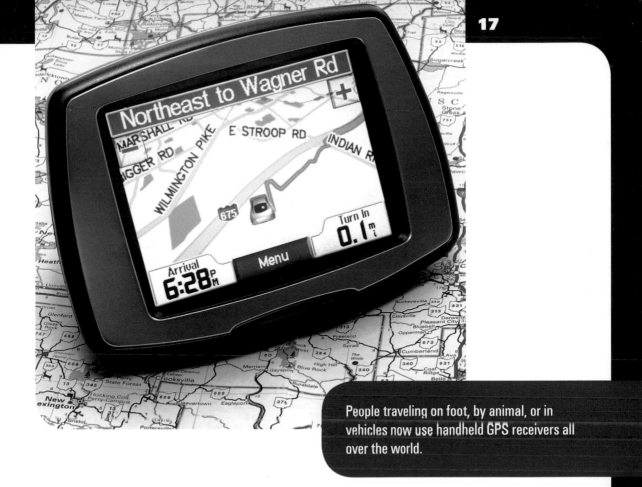

People traveling on foot, by animal, or in vehicles now use handheld GPS receivers all over the world.

Many new ideas cost a lot of money to develop. Sometimes it can be less expensive to adapt technology created for other purposes. Global Positioning System (GPS) receivers, for example, were first used in submarines. They helped submarines **navigate** better underwater. GPS systems were added to airplanes to help pilots navigate the skies. These systems use signals from satellites. The first GPS receivers cost thousands of dollars. Today, they can cost as little as $100. And they are not just used in airplanes anymore. You may even have one in your cell phone!

21st Century Content

Years ago, no one would have ever dreamed that people would one day be living in airport cities. Does living in an aerotropolis sound like fun? Think about going to a school at an international airport. Imagine how many students from different parts of the world there would be. What things would be similar to the school you go to now? What things would be different?

With so many people and goods traveling by air, more airports will need to be built and more workers will be needed. In addition to runways and terminals, new airports have started to include mini-cities called aerotropolises. They include grocery stores, office buildings, parks, theaters, and even schools.

Workers live in these mini-cities so they don't have to travel to get to work each day. Business travelers can stay in hotels there and conduct their business right at the airport.

The first aerotropolis was built in Amsterdam, Holland. Dubai World Central, an aerotropolis being built in Dubai, United Arab Emirates, will be the world's largest. It is estimated that 750,000 people will live there.

CHAPTER FOUR

The Future for Airplanes

Imagine flying in an airplane that does not have a pilot on board! Or an airplane that can travel across the United States in the same amount of time as your lunch period. These new ideas for airplanes of the future might sound impossible, but they may be just around the corner. Today, there are already unmanned airplanes controlled by

The U.S. Air Force uses unmanned aircraft, such as the RQ-4 Global Hawk (above).

Life & Career Skills

In 1894, a scientist named Octave Chanute said one of the best ideas he ever had was to invent a flying machine. He had three reasons he thought this was a good idea.

The first reason was because flying would save time when traveling long distances. Second, a flying machine would make it possible for people to go anywhere in the world. Third, meeting and working with new cultures would require people to learn how to live peacefully with other groups. Chanute was right. These are just a few of the many reasons why we fly airplanes today.

What is the best idea you ever had? Why did you think it was a good idea? Share your idea with others. Working toward a shared goal with others can be one of the best ways to turn an idea into a successful innovation.

computers being used for military operations in areas too dangerous for humans.

Engineers continue to try to figure out ways to make air travel faster. They think about how to create engines that can produce bigger blasts of power. They imagine that these more powerful engines will allow airplanes to travel from Canada to Mexico in just 30 minutes!

Not all airplane innovations are about making things bigger or faster. The Federal Aviation Administration (FAA) is looking for different power sources for airplanes. Imagine an airplane that uses fuel made from corn instead of oil. Imagine a battery the size of your hand supplying all the electrical power for a passenger jet!

Airplanes of the future will need to use less fuel and make less noise. Engineers and aviators all over the world are working

The wheels on this commercial airliner are lowered before landing.

to make these ideas a reality. Until then, airplanes will continue to help travelers connect with people all over the world.

Some Famous Aviation Innovators

Airplanes are the safest and quickest way to travel today. But one person alone could not have developed airplanes. The following is a list of people whose curiosity, determination, passion, and persistence helped make airplanes a great mode of transportation.

Wilbur and Orville Wright

Both Wilbur and Orville Wright were shy, curious boys. Instead of going to college, they opened a shop to build bicycles in Dayton, Ohio. Soon they became more interested in building a powered airplane than building bicycles. The brothers spent four years watching birds, flying kites, and building and testing gliders. They used research from scientist Samuel P. Langley to help them figure out what they needed to do. Most

Orville Wright made the first successful flight of the powered, controlled airplane that he and his brother built. The flight lasted 12 seconds.

people thought they were crazy, calling them "the Buzzard boys."

After many, many failures, they succeeded! On December 17, 1903, Orville made the first manned, heavier-than-air, powered flight at Kitty Hawk, North Carolina. The Wright brothers continued experimenting with new ideas to improve their airplane. They believed airplanes would make life better for people everywhere.

Igor Sikorsky stands in front of a flying boat, which was built by his company, in 1936.

Igor Sikorsky

Igor Sikorsky was a homeschooled student in Kiev, Russia (now the capital of Ukraine). He began making flying machine models by looking at pictures of flying machines drawn by 15th-century Italian artist Leonardo da Vinci.

In 1906, Sikorsky saw a photo in a newspaper of Orville Wright and his airplane. Sikorsky was determined to build large airplanes that could carry many people across great distances. Seven years later, he built his first four-engine airplane.

Sikorsky **immigrated** to the United States in 1919. He formed a company and built airplanes called flying boats. These huge four-engine airplanes became the first to carry passengers across the Atlantic Ocean for Pan American Airways. In 1939, he built one of the world's first successful helicopters. It looked very much like the drawings of one of Leonardo da Vinci's flying machines that he had studied as a boy.

William P. "Bill" Lear

Bill Lear grew up in Hannibal, Missouri. He combined his interest in cars and electronics to invent the first car radio in 1930. The car radio became an instant success!

Lear was passionate about flying. At the beginning of World War II, he combined a compass with electronic radio signals and invented the first airplane radio compass. This instrument allowed pilots to find their directions using signals from radio towers. It was so successful that Lear invented an entire system of electronic instruments known as the automatic pilot system.

Electronic instruments in airplanes completely changed how planes were flown. Today, pilots all over the world use electronic instruments to assure airplanes take off correctly, stay exactly on course, and land safely.

Clarence "Kelly" Johnson

Clarence "Kelly" Johnson won a prize for his first airplane design when he was a 13-year-old student in Ishpeming, Michigan. After college, he spent more than 40 years as an airplane engineer. He was placed in charge of all airplanes planned, built, and tested in a place known as the Lockheed "Skunk Works."

C. L. "Kelly" Johnson helped design more than 40 Lockheed aircraft, including the F-104 Starfighter (above).

Johnson earned almost every award given for airplane innovations. However, he never forgot the first prize he won while he was a student. He said it inspired him to be persistent.

Elbert L. "Burt" Rutan

Burt Rutan's big brother, Dick, would not let Burt play with his model airplanes when they were growing up in California. So Burt began building his own models. He and Dick got their mom to drive them late at night on country roads while they held their airplane models outside the car windows. They wanted to see how well their designs would fly.

Burt earned a college degree in aeronautical engineering. He worked for the United States Air Force solving problems other engineers could not solve. He had so many new ideas that he started his own company, known as Scaled Composites, Inc., to design and develop aircraft using lightweight materials. *Voyager* is the most famous airplane he designed and built. It was the first airplane to fly successfully nonstop around the world without being refueled. It made the record-setting nine-day flight in 1986 piloted by Dick Rutan and Jeana Yeager.

Throughout his career, Burt Rutan's curiosity has helped him find things that need improving in airplanes and figure out how to make them better.

In 1932, Amelia Earhart became the first woman to fly solo nonstop across the Atlantic Ocean. She was inspired by women pilots who had made long-distance flights alone in other parts of the world.

Amelia Earhart

Amelia Earhart was one of the greatest aviators of all time. She broke the women's altitude record in 1922, flying up to 14,000 feet (4,300 meters). She was also the first woman to fly successfully over the Atlantic Ocean in 1928. Aside from being a world-class aviator, Earhart was a women's rights activist. She helped form The Ninety-Nines, an organization of female pilots.

In 1937, while trying to fly around the globe, her aircraft mysteriously disappeared over the Pacific Ocean. To this day, no one knows what happened to this trailblazing female aviator.

Charles Lindbergh poses in an open cockpit biplane. He flew different kinds of airplanes to decide what style would be best for the *Spirit of St. Louis*.

Charles Lindbergh

Charles Lindbergh is one of the most famous American aviators of all time. In 1927, he became the first pilot to fly solo nonstop across the Atlantic Ocean. The flight was from May 20 to May 21. After the historic flight, he continued to fly and served as a consultant for the U.S. Air Force.

Glossary

cultures (KUHL-churz) the shared beliefs, actions, and traits of social groups

English Channel (ING-lesh CHA-nuhl) narrow part of the Atlantic Ocean between England and France

global (GLOHB-uhl) the whole world

hydrogen (HY-droh-juhn) a colorless, odorless gas

immigrated (IM-uh-grayt-id) came to a country where you were not born

navigate (NAV-uh-gate) to steer a course through the air

patent (PAT-uhnt) a legal document giving an inventor the sole rights to manufacture and sell his or her invention

propeller (pruh-PEL-ur) a blade turned by an engine to pull an airplane through the air

terminal (TUR-muh-nuhl) a building at an airport for passengers to use between flights

transport (transs-PORT) move from one place to another

For More Information

BOOKS

Bingham, Caroline. *Airplane*. New York: DK Publishing, 2006.

Masters, Nancy Robinson. *Airplanes*. Ann Arbor, MI: Cherry Lake Publishing, 2008.

Sandler, Martin W. *Flying Over the USA: Airplanes in American Life*. New York: Oxford University Press, 2004.

WEB SITES

AvKids.com
www.avkids.com/hangar
For aviation games and other activities

EAA Young Eagles
www.youngeagles.org/
Learn more about this program for kids interested in aviation

Index

About the Author

Nancy Robinson Masters is an airplane pilot who lives in Texas. She is also an author who loves to write about new ideas and inventions. She travels all over the world to visit schools and talk with students about innovations. She says, "Reading and writing skills are very, very important. Every innovator needs to be a good communicator!" Nancy is the author of more than 20 books, including *Jeans*, *Salt*, and *Airplanes* in the Cherry Lake Publishing Global Products series for middle school readers.